I'm Bold!

Zolani Overcomes His Fears

Published by LoveWorld Publishing Limited
3, Adebayo Akande Street, Oregun, Ikeja,
Lagos, Nigeria.
E-mail: info@loveworldbooks.org, info@kiddiesloveworld.org
Website: www.loveworldpublishing.org

ISBN: 978-1-946026-31-6

Copyright © 2019 by LoveWorld Publishing.

All rights reserved under International Copyright Law.
Contents and/or cover may not be reproduced in whole or in part in any form without the express written permission of LoveWorld Publishing.

Scripture taken from the New King James Version®.
Copyright © 1982 by Thomas Nelson, Inc. Used by permission. All rights reserved.

FOR MORE INFORMATION AND TO PLACE ORDERS:

UNITED KINGDOM:
Unit C2, Thames View Business Center,
Barlow Way Rainham-Essex,
RM 13 8BT.
Tel.: +44 (0) 1708 556 604
Fax: + 44 (0) 2081 816 290

USA:
4237 Raleigh Street
Charlotte, NC 28213
Tel.: +1 980-219-5150

USA:
Christ Embassy Houston,
8623 Hemlock Hill Drive
Houston, Texas. 77083
Tel.: +1-281-759-5111
      +1-281-759-6218

CANADA:
4101 Steeles Ave W,
Suite 204, Toronto, Ontario,
Canada M3N 1V7

SOUTH AFRICA:
303 Pretoria Avenue
Cnr. Harley and Braam Fischer,
Randburg, Gauteng
South Africa.
Tel.: +27 11 326 0971
Fax: +27 113260972

NIGERIA:
Christ Embassy
Plot 97 Durumi District, Abuja,
Nigeria.

LoveWorld Conference Center
Kudirat Abiola Way, Oregun
P.O. Box 13563 Ikeja, Lagos.
Tel.: +234-812-340-6547
      +234-812-340-6791

"For God has not given us a spirit of fear, but of power and of love and of a sound mind"

(2 Timothy 1:7).

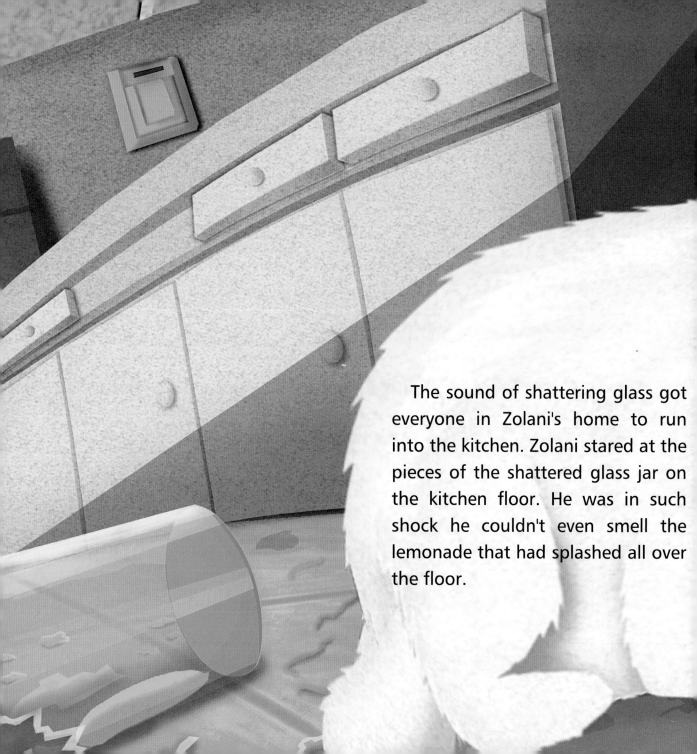

The sound of shattering glass got everyone in Zolani's home to run into the kitchen. Zolani stared at the pieces of the shattered glass jar on the kitchen floor. He was in such shock he couldn't even smell the lemonade that had splashed all over the floor.

"What happened here?" his father asked.

Zolani was still in shock to utter a word.

"Zolani, are you alright?" His mother asked as she led him out of the kitchen.

"Oh no! There goes our lemonade!" Thato, Zolani's elder brother said.

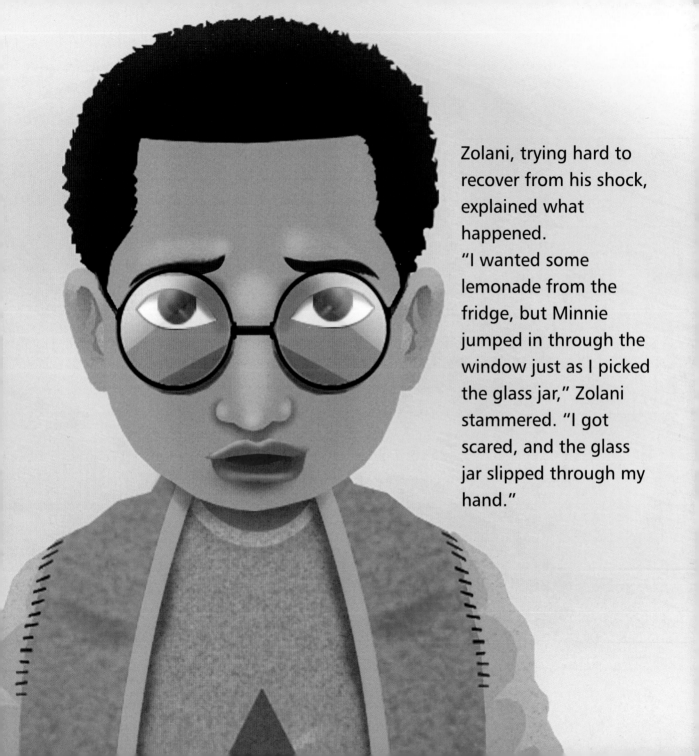

Zolani, trying hard to recover from his shock, explained what happened.
"I wanted some lemonade from the fridge, but Minnie jumped in through the window just as I picked the glass jar," Zolani stammered. "I got scared, and the glass jar slipped through my hand."

"Your mother is right, Thato." Zolani's father said. "Don't call Zolani a *scaredy cat*. By the way, Thato, it's time for your soccer practice. We mustn't be late."

"Ok, Pa," Thato replied as he dashed off to get his training kit.

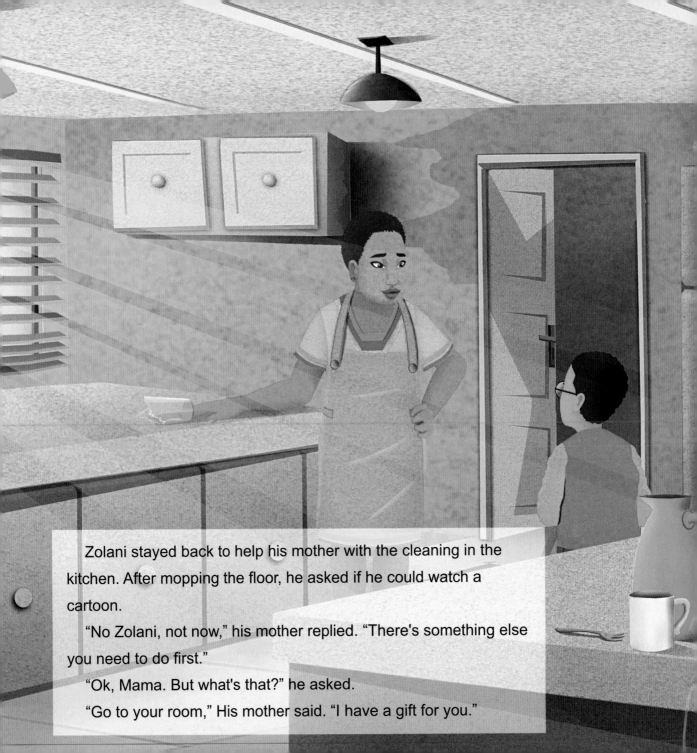

Zolani stayed back to help his mother with the cleaning in the kitchen. After mopping the floor, he asked if he could watch a cartoon.

"No Zolani, not now," his mother replied. "There's something else you need to do first."

"Ok, Mama. But what's that?" he asked.

"Go to your room," His mother said. "I have a gift for you."

Zolani's mother went to fetch the gift from her room. It was a book.

"I want you to read this book," she said. "Your Aunt Adowa got it just for you."

Zolani collected the book and looked at it. A flash of excitement beamed through his eyes as he slowly read the title, *"My Faith Book of Confessions."*

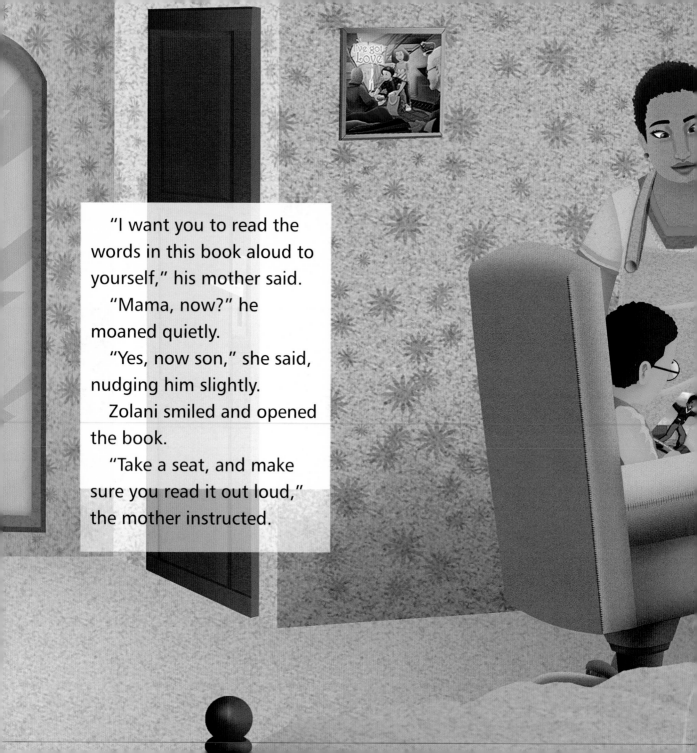

"I want you to read the words in this book aloud to yourself," his mother said.

"Mama, now?" he moaned quietly.

"Yes, now son," she said, nudging him slightly.

Zolani smiled and opened the book.

"Take a seat, and make sure you read it out loud," the mother instructed.

As his mother left for the kitchen, Zolani opened the book and began to read it. It wasn't long before he began to say the words aloud.

"I'm bold! I'm courageous! The greater One lives in me! I'm a child of God!"

Later that day, Zolani's mother asked him to run an errand for her.

"I have a basket of fruits for Mama Rosa," she said. "Could you take it to her for me?"

Mama Rosa was their next door neighbour.

The children in Zolani's neighbourhood were scared of Mama Rosa. They believed she had a wicked stick she's always holding that turned children into rats. So, none of them ever dared to get close to her door.

"Mama Rosa?" Zolani shook his head. "Please don't send me to Mama Rosa. She has a wicked stick that turns children into rats. I'm not going there."

Zolani's mother laughed at her son.

"Zolani, Mama Rosa can't turn children into rats. And even if she could, it won't be my Zolani, the bold child of Almighty God. Or aren't you?"

"Y-yes, I am!" Zolani stuttered.

Zolani was quiet for a while as he thought about what his mother said.

"Zolani," his mother called, "does the greater One really live in you?"

At that moment, Zolani remembered what he had read a few hours earlier.

"Yes, the greater One lives in me, Mama," Zolani replied boldly.

"Are you sure?" His mother quizzed him to be sure if he would go on the errand.

"Yes, I am, Mama," Zolani said with confidence.

Then, he decided to run the errand for his mother.

"Where's the fruit basket Mama?" Zolani asked. "I'll take it to Mama Rosa for you."

His mother handed him the basket. "There you go, my bold son! Give my regards to Mama Rosa."

Zolani carried the basket and headed to Mama Rosa's house. He got to the door and knocked. His heart beat faster. But as he confessed the words he read from ***"My Faith Book of Confessions,"*** he became confident and bold.

As he heard footsteps coming near the door, he expected it to open, but it didn't. He waited patiently. Sweat droplets ran from his forehead to his cheeks.

"Who's there?" Mama Rosa's cracked voice bellow out.

Although her voice was loud and harsh, Zolani was not scared anymore. The sweat drops had dried, the thumping of his heart had stopped. He was calm and confident.

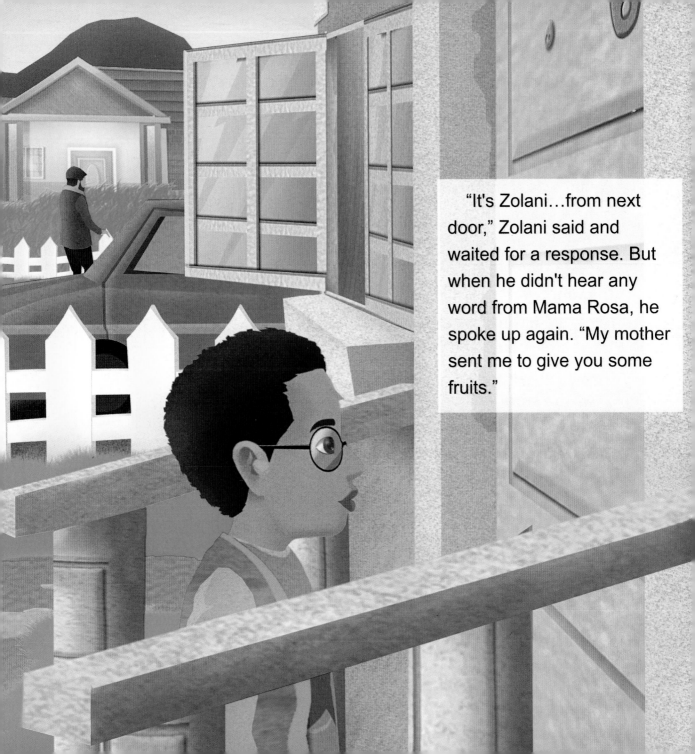

"It's Zolani…from next door," Zolani said and waited for a response. But when he didn't hear any word from Mama Rosa, he spoke up again. "My mother sent me to give you some fruits."

Mama Rosa's door swung open and Zolani was standing face-to-face before Mama Rosa.

She was an old brown-skinned woman. Her silver hair, though thinning, were neatly packed, making her wrinkled forehead more obvious. She barely could see without the help of her round glasses.

As she stooped over to have a closer look at her visitor, Zolani observed the cane in her wrinkled dry hand.

"She doesn't have a stick that turns children into rats," Zolani thought to himself. "It's only a walking cane."

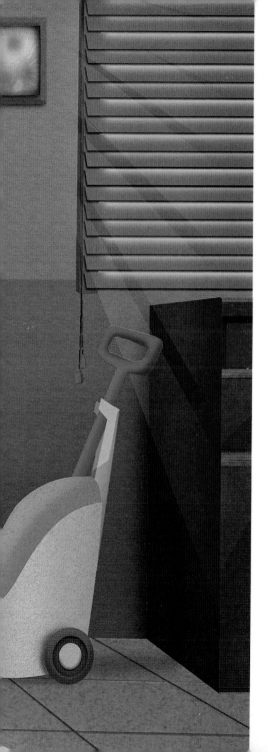

"Hello Zolani. It's nice to see you," Mama Rosa said. "Thank you for bringing me the basket of fruits."

"You're welcome, Mama," Zolani replied.

"Would you be kind enough to place them on the table in my kitchen?" Mama Rosa requested.

"Why the kitchen?" A thought ran through Zolani's mind. "Could this be a trap? Why wouldn't she collect the basket from me here? Why is she asking me into her house?"

But he stopped the thoughts with the right confession. "I know who I am; I'm bold, I have a sound mind!" He whispered to himself again.

Suddenly, the fearful thoughts left him.

Zolani stepped into Mama Rosa's house and placed the fruits on the kitchen table.

"Thank you, my son," Mama Rosa said.

"You're welcome Mama," Zolani replied again.

As he turned to leave, he faced Mama Rosa and said, "You're not terrible; you're actually a kind person."

"Oh my boy, do you really believe those funny tales your friends made up about me?" Mama Rosa smiled. "I don't harm children. Your mother knows that too, otherwise, she wouldn't have sent you to my place. And if you hadn't come, you wouldn't have found out for yourself."

Mama Rosa brought out a pack of sweets from her refrigerator.

"Here's a small reward for being bold Zolani," Mama Rosa said as she handed them to Zolani. "You can share some of these candies with your brother and your friends."

"Thank you, Mama Rosa!" Zolani said and went home happily.

"Mama, I saw Mama Rosa," Zolani said excitedly. "She doesn't turn children into rats. She's very kind; she asked me to thank you for the fruits."

"Really?" His mother said teasingly.

"Yes-yes, Mama," Zolani said, still very excited. "See, she gave me a pack of sweets for being bold."

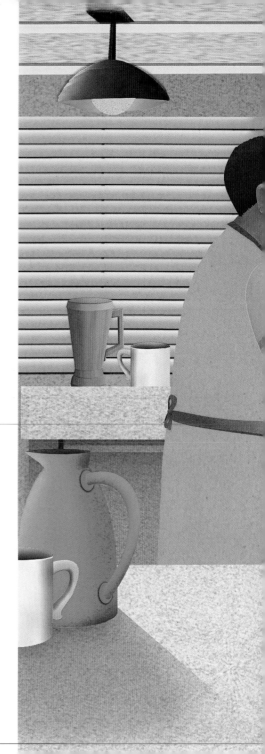

"Wow!" His mother exclaimed. "My Zolani went to Mama Rosa and came back with a pack of sweets for being bold. That's wonderful! Do you see how speaking God's Word can change your life?"

"Yes Mama," Zolani said. "I have the life of God in me. I'm not scared anymore. I'm bold!"

Zolani hugged his mother.

"Thank you for teaching me how to be bold Mama," Zolani said. "Can I have some lemonade now?"

"Sure, you can," his mother replied.

Just about the time
Zolani's mother was
pouring the lemonade in
a glass, Minnie showed
up again at the window.
Zolani and his mother
looked at each other and
giggled.
"May I pour Minnie
some milk?" Zolani
asked.

"That's up to you," Zolani's mother said.

Zolani brought out a milk jar from the refrigerator and poured some milk into Minnie's bowl.

Minnie walked to the bowl and lapped it.

Zolani patted Minnie on the head, and it purred.

Zolani and his mother looked at each other and giggled again.

"I can see God's Spirit has really given you boldness," Zolani's mother teased him.

"Yes Mama," Zolani said confidently. "I'm no longer afraid of Minnie the cat or Mama Rosa. I won't even be scared when I'm alone in my room, and it's dark and raining.

"That's great," Zolani's mother applauded him. "That's why the Bible says in 2 Timothy 1:7, 'For God has not given us a spirit of fear, but of power and of love and of a sound mind.'"

"Thank you again, Mama," Zolani said and hugged his mother. "God's Spirit lives in me. Therefore, I'm bold."

What The Bible Says

God wants you to be bold at all time and in any situation. Here are some scripture verses to read and memorise; they'll help your confidence.

- *"So we may boldly say: 'The Lord is my helper; I will not fear. What can man do to me?'"* (Hebrews 13:6).

- *"There is no fear in love. But perfect love drives out fear…"* (1John 4:18).

- *"For God has not given us a spirit of fear, but of power and of love and of a sound mind."* (2 Timothy 1:7).

- *"Don't be afraid of anyone …"* (Matthew 10:26 CEV).

- *"'Have courage!' Jesus immediately told them. "It's me. Stop being afraid!"* (Matthew 14:27 ISV).

- *"Do not be afraid, little flock, for your Father has been pleased to give you the kingdom"* (Luke 12:32 NIV).

- *"The wicked run away when no one is chasing them, but the godly are as bold as lions"* (Proverbs 28:1 NLT).

- *"When I called, you answered me; you made me bold and stouthearted"* (Psalm 138:3 NIV).

- *"Then Paul and Barnabas grew bold and said, "It was necessary that the word of God should be spoken to you first…."* (Act 13:46).

A Lesson For You

Kick Fear Out!

As a child of God, the Lord doesn't want you living in fear. No! You shouldn't let anyone or anything scare you; whether it's a thunderstorm or darkness.

Fear is not from God, it's from the devil. So, don't let it stay in you. God has made you righteous and "the righteous are bold as a lion" (Proverbs 28:1). Hallelujah!

You're God's precious child and He'll never let anyone or anything harm you. So be bold and refuse to fear. Remember you have the love of God in you and "...perfect love casts out fear" (1 John 4:18). Praise God! The next time fear shows up, kick it out with God's Word by declaring, "The greater One, Christ, lives in me, therefore, fear get out, now," and it will be as you have said. Hallelujah!

Say This Prayer

I'm bold. There's no fear in me for I'm full of courage and God's love!

RORK LIBRARY©

ORDER NOW!

GREAT MIRACLES of the BIBLE

A **3- in -1** storybook with
BOLD BEAUTIFUL ILLUSTRATIONS
and easy to read font style.

Great Miracles of the Bible is a collection of inspiring illustrated stories of God's divine intervention in the affairs of men that would stir children to have faith in God and the miraculous. This edition has three exciting stories and themes with vivid illustrations. As an added feature, we have included Discussion/ Q&A pages help strengthen what they will learn in each story, building in them life principles.

To Order: Call: NIG: +234-812-340-6547; +234-812-340-6791
UK: +44 (0) 1708 556 604, SA: +27 11 326 0971
USA: +1 980-219-5150, +1-281-759-5111; +1-281-759-6218
Or send E-mail: info@loveworldbooks.org, info@kiddiesloveworld.org
Visit Website: www.loveworldpublishing.org

My Faith Confessions!

Keep saying it! Don't
stop talking it!!
Start the kids out right
and help them develop
the habit of confessing
the Word of God.
My Faith Confessions series
tailored specifically
for kids and Pre-Teens,
is the right place
to start!

**Makes Great Gift
For Every Child!**

ORDER NOW!

To Order: Call: NIG: +234-812-340-6547; +234-812-340-6791
UK: +44 (0) 1708 556 604, SA: +27 11 326 0971
USA: +1 980-219-5150, +1-281-759-5111; +1-281-759-6218
Or send E-mail: info@loveworldbooks.org, info@kiddiesloveworld.org
Visit Website: www.loveworldpublishing.org

6 Great books to Have!

Children can live victoriously every day once they know what they've got inside them. Help them discover who they really are in Christ with these interesting story books from the "*I Know Who I Am Collection*", and watch them grow to become who God intended them to be.

To Order: **Call: NIG: +234-812-340-6547; +234-812-340-6791**
UK: +44 (0) 1708 556 604, SA: +27 11 326 0971
USA: +1 980-219-5150, +1-281-759-5111; +1-281-759-6218
Or send E-mail: info@loveworldbooks.org, info@kiddiesloveworld.org
Visit Website: www.loveworldpublishing.org

CHILDREN'S BOOKS

About the Book

Zolani Kiran is so timid that everything frightens him. He's scared to sleep alone at night, he's scared of thunder and lightning. He's so scared that even Minnie, the family cat, frightens him.

His mother sends him to their neighbour, Mama Rosa, to drop a basket of fruits. He is scared to go to Mama Rosa's house because his friends told him she has a wicked stick that turns children into rats.

Will Zolani be bold enough to knock on Mama Rosa's door? Find out in the story.

About the Author

Pastor Chris Oyakhilome is the President of LoveWorld Inc. He is a dedicated Minister of God's Word whose messages have brought the reality of the Christian life to many around the world, including children.

Millions of people have been blessed by his television programmes, crusades, as well as books for both adults and children.

Through his dedication to God's Word, thousands of churches have been established worldwide.

£99
I'm recycled ♻ age UK

LoveWorld Publishing

ISBN 978-1-946026-31-6

9 781946 026316